Cesar Chavez

A Photo-Illustrated Biography
by Lucile Davis

Content Consultants:
Helen Chavez, President
Monica Parra, Administrator
Cesar E. Chavez Foundation

Bridgestone Books

an imprint of Capstone Press

Fast Facts about Cesar Chavez

- Cesar Chavez was a farm worker from age 4 to age 35.
- He was against using violence to solve problems.
- He founded the first union for farm workers in the United States.
- He was awarded the Presidential Medal of Freedom.

Bridgestone Books are published by Capstone Press
151 Good Counsel Drive, P.O. Box 669, Mankato, Minnesota 56002
http://www.capstone-press.com

Library of Congress Cataloging-in-Publication Data
Davis, Lucile.
    Cesar Chavez: a photo-illustrated biography / by Lucile Davis.
    p. cm.
    Includes bibliographical references and index.
    Summary: Presents the life story of the Mexican American labor leader who achieved justice for migrant farm workers by creating a union to protect their rights.
    ISBN 1-56065-569-0
    1. Chavez, Cesar, 1927– —Juvenile literature. 2. United Farm Workers—History—Juvenile literature. 3. National Farm Workers Association—History—Juvenile literature. 4. Labor leaders—United States—Biography—Juvenile literature. 5. Mexican-American migrant agricultural laborers—Biography—Juvenile literature. 6. Trade-unions—Migrant agricultural laborers—United States—History—Juvenile literature. 7. Mexican Americans—Biography—Juvenile literature. [1. Chavez, Cesar, 1927–. 2. Labor leaders. 3. Mexican Americans—Biography. 4. United Farm Workers—History.] I. Chavez, Cesar, 1927–. II. Title.
HD6509.C48D38   1998
331.88′13′092—dc21   97-5176
[B]   CIP
                                                                                               AC

The quotes on page 22 are courtesy of the Cesar E. Chavez Foundation.

Photo Credits
Archive Photos, cover; Archives of Labor and Urban Affairs, Wayne State University, 6, 8, 10, 16, 18; Corbis-Bettman, 4, 14, 20; UPI/Corbis-Bettman, 12

Table of Contents

Union Leader

Cesar Chavez spent most of his life trying to help farm workers. He knew about their hard lives. Once he had worked in the fields, too. Cesar started a union called the United Farm Workers. A union seeks fair treatment and better pay for workers.

Cesar was a gentle man. He did not believe in using violence. Violence is the use of force. Cesar traveled all over California to hear farm workers' problems. The workers listened when Cesar talked about the union.

Cesar brought attention to the problems of farm workers. He led marches and strikes. A strike is when a group stops working until conditions are changed. Cesar also asked people not to buy things from certain companies. This is called a boycott. Cesar led boycotts against companies that treated workers badly.

Cesar led strikes to bring attention to farm workers' problems.

Growing Up

Cesar Chavez was born in Arizona on March 31, 1927. He was named after his grandfather, Cesario. Cesario worked on a farm in Mexico. He was treated like a slave there. A slave is a person who is owned by someone else. Cesario escaped to Arizona with his family in 1888.

Cesar's parents owned a farm in Arizona. His father's name was Librado. Librado also ran a grocery store. Cesar's mother's name was Juana. She watched over the family.

Juana gave good advice. She told her children not to fight. Librado taught Cesar helpful lessons. Librado said people should stand up for themselves and for others.

Cesar grew up in a happy home. He went to school. But he did not like it much. Cesar played with his brothers and sisters. They all helped with the farm work.

Cesar was named after his grandfather, Cesario.

California Farm Worker

Cesar's family lost their farm and store in 1937. This was during the Great Depression (1929-1939). The depression was a period of hard times when many people were poor. Thousands of people lost their jobs.

The Chavez family moved to California to find work. They found that farm workers were paid very little. They had to live in one-room shacks. Everyone in the family had to work long hours. They spent their days working hard to pick crops.

The family traveled from one farm to another to find work. They moved on when a crop had been picked. The Chavez family had little money. Life as farm workers was hard.

The Chavez children went to school when they could. They also tried to help the family. The boys fished and hunted for food. The girls picked wild plants to eat.

Cesar's family lost their farm in Arizona during the Great Depression.

School and the Navy

In 1939, the Chavez family settled in Sal Si Puedes, California. In Spanish, the name of the town means get out if you can. Juana and Librado did any work they could find. The children went to school.

Then Librado was hurt in a car crash. Cesar had to quit school to help his family. He only finished eighth grade. After that, he worked full-time.

Cesar began dating Helen Fabela when he was 15 years old. They dated for two years. Then Cesar joined the United States Navy in 1944. He worked on a ship.

Cesar returned home after his service was over. He and Helen were married in 1948. She gave birth to their first child, Fernando Chavez, the next year. Over the years, they had seven more children.

Cesar married Helen Fabela in 1948.

Helping Farm Workers

Cesar went back to working in the fields. Conditions for farm workers were still very bad. Cesar wanted to change things.

He began to read books about leaders. He learned how some leaders made life better for others. In 1952, Cesar started working for the Community Service Organization. This group helped Mexican Americans in California. Cesar helped people sign up to vote. He taught them about their rights.

In Oxnard, California, farm workers told Cesar they could not get jobs. Farm owners were hiring workers from Mexico instead. This was against the law. Cesar made the government look into the problem. Finally, the owners agreed to hire local workers. Cesar had made a difference. But he wanted to help more.

Cesar started working for the Community Service Organization in 1952.

Organizing the Union

Cesar believed that farm workers needed a union. Other kinds of workers had unions. Union workers joined together to fight for their rights. A union could help farm workers receive better treatment and better pay. The workers would go on strike if farm owners refused to change conditions. Cesar decided to start a union. He quit his job.

Cesar went from town to town. He talked to farm workers about the union. In 1962, Cesar held the first meeting of the National Farm Workers Association. They later changed the name to the United Farm Workers. It was the first union for farm workers in the United States.

The union's saying was Viva La Causa. This means Long Live the Cause. Cesar got many people to join the union. He also started looking for ways to help workers.

Cesar started a union to help farm workers receive better treatment and better pay.

Strike and Boycott

Farm owners in California were treating their grape pickers badly. In 1965, farm owners cut the workers' pay. Cesar led his union's first strike. The grape pickers went on strike with Cesar's union.

The farm owners became angry. Crops rotted in the fields. The owners lost money. Sometimes the owners sent men to beat the farm workers. Cesar remembered his mother's words about not fighting. He told the workers to be peaceful.

Cesar wanted people to know how grape pickers were treated. So he started a boycott. Cesar asked everyone to stop buying grapes. He asked grocery stores not to sell grapes. Many people supported the boycott. The truck drivers' union stopped carrying grapes in their trucks. Another union refused to unload grapes from ships.

Cesar started strikes and boycotts to help grape pickers. He asked everyone to stop buying grapes.

Victory

The boycott and the strike helped. Conditions for farm workers got a little better. But Cesar wanted more people to know about the workers' problems. He hoped people would help the workers.

In 1966, Cesar led a march to Sacramento, California. The march gained the attention of the government and the public. It was a peaceful way to ask for change.

The grape pickers' strike continued for years. Cesar went on a fast in 1968. A fast is when someone stops eating for a time. Cesar did not eat for 25 days. He fasted to show workers how to be strong and peaceful.

It took five years for the grape growers to change. But finally Cesar and the workers won. The grape growers raised the workers' pay. They agreed to work with the union to make conditions better. The grape pickers went back to work.

Cesar led a peaceful march to Sacramento, California. The march called attention to farm workers' problems.

The Work Continues

Cesar knew many farm workers still needed help. He led more marches and boycotts.

Cesar wanted to stop the use of pesticides. Pesticides are chemicals used to protect crops. Some pesticides made workers sick. In 1988, Cesar went on another fast to bring attention to the problem. This fast lasted for 36 days.

Cesar traveled. He wanted everyone to know about and help the farm workers. He gained support for the farm workers' cause. People all over the world began to support the workers.

Cesar worked for the union for the rest of his life. He died on April 23, 1993, in Arizona. In 1994, Cesar was awarded the Presidential Medal of Freedom. The medal honors people who help others. Cesar's wife, Helen, accepted the medal for him.

Cesar's life became an example of how to help people. Many people are continuing the work that Cesar began.

Cesar wanted to stop the use of pesticides. The pesticides made farm workers sick.

Words from Cesar Chavez

"Being of service is not enough. You must become a servant of the people."

From Cesar Chavez' Commitment Speech.

"The end of all education should surely be service to others. Students must have initiative, they should not be mere imitators. They must learn to think and act for themselves and be free."

From Cochelle - "Dedication of the Heart."

"Our lives are all that really belong to us. So it is how we use our lives that determines what kind of men we are."

From Cesar's speech after ending his fast in 1968.

Important Dates in Cesar Chavez's Life

1927—Born on March 31 in Arizona

1937—Family loses farm and store and moves to California

1942—Finishes eighth grade

1944—Joins the U.S. Navy

1948—Marries Helen Fabela

1962—Starts the United Farm Workers

1965—Grape pickers' strike begins

1966—Leads nationwide boycott of grapes; leads march to Sacramento

1968—Goes on first hunger strike

1970—Grape growers give in to the union

1993—Dies on April 23 in Arizona

1994—Awarded Presidential Medal of Freedom

Words to Know

boycott (BOI-kot)—to refuse to buy things from a company

Great Depression (GRAYT di-PRESH-uhn)—a period of hard times from 1929 to 1939 in the United States when many people lost their jobs

pesticide (PESS-tih-side)—a chemical used to protect crops

strike (STRIKE)—when a group of workers stop working until conditions are changed

union (YOON-yuhn)—a group of workers who join together to seek fair treatment and better pay

violence (VYE-uh-luhnss)—the use of force

Read More

Altman, Linda Jacobs. *Cesar Chavez.* San Diego: Lucent Books, 1996.
Collins, David. *Farmworker's Friend: The Story of Cesar Chavez.*
Minneapolis: Carolrhoda Books, 1996.
Holmes, Burnham. *Cesar Chavez: Farm Worker Activist.* Austin, Texas:
Raintree Steck-Vaughn, 1994.

Useful Addresses and Internet Sites

Cesar E. Chavez Collection
Michigan State University
100 Library
East Lansing, MI 48824-1048

Cesar E. Chavez Foundation
P.O. Box 62
Keene, CA 93531

Cesar Chavez: Farm Union Organizer
http://www.who2.com/cesarchavez.html
Cesar Chavez School; Chavez Biography
http://www.oxnardsd.org/campus/chav/chavez.html
Cesar E. Chavez Homepage
http://thecity.sfsu.edu/~ccipp/cecresources.html

Index